ELEANOR ROOSEVELT

ELEANOR ROOSEVELT

First Lady of the Twentieth Century
by Ted Gottfried

A Book Report Biography
FRANKLIN WATTS
A Division of Grolier Publishing
New York London Hong Kong Sydney
Danbury, Connecticut

In memory of my mother,
Jennie Bach Gottfried.
"Three things to remember," she said.
"Never mistreat a dog. Never trust a landlord.
Never lose faith in Eleanor Roosevelt!"

Photographs ©: Archive Photos/Popperfoto: 38; Brown Brothers: 41, 64, 91; Corbis-Bettmann: 2, 20, 22, 77; Franklin D. Roosevelt Library: 29, 32, 40, 45, 49, 53, 58, 66, 72, 74, 89; United Nations: 100; UPI/Corbis-Bettmann: 17, 75, 81, 87, 95, 97.

Gottfried, Ted.
    Eleanor Roosevelt: First Lady of the Twentieth Century / Ted Gottfried.
        p. cm.—(A book report biography)
    Includes bibliographical references and index.
    ISBN 0-531-11406-6
    1. Roosevelt, Eleanor, 1884–1962—Juvenile literature. 2. Presidents' spouses—United States—Biography—Juvenile literature. I. Title. II. Series.
        E807.1.R48G67 1997
        973.917'092—dc21
        [B]   96-49314
                                                                 CIP
                                                                  AC

CONTENTS

ACKNOWLEDGMENTS

I am indebted to the following people for their support on this book: Abe Kobrin for providing long-lost research material; author Janet Bode for her young-adult expertise; Kathryn Paulsen for file cabinets and never-failing ego-building support; the personnel of various branches of the New York Public Library, and, as always, my librarian wife, Harriet Gottfried, who read and critiqued the manuscript in progress. Their help was invaluable, but any errors or shortcomings are mine alone.

CHAPTER ONE

THE MOST ADMIRED WOMAN

"The most admired woman in the United States"—that's how the American people rated Eleanor Roosevelt in a Gallup Poll taken in 1958. She was 73 years old at the time. It had been 13 years since her husband, President Franklin Roosevelt, had died. She was no longer the nation's First Lady, but her popularity had endured. Almost 40 years later, in 1996, another First Lady, Hillary Rodham Clinton, told reporters that she had long looked up to Eleanor Roosevelt as a role model. That has been true of many women since Eleanor Roosevelt first entered public life, and it still is. Eleanor Roosevelt endures as a shining example to women today, just as she was to the women of her time.

Mrs. Roosevelt was modest about being so admired. She thought that the only lesson her life might offer was "to show that one can, even without any particular gifts, overcome obstacles . . . . that, in spite of timidity and fear, in spite of a lack of special talents, one can find a way to live widely and fully." It was what she did once she had overcome those obstacles that gained her the love and admiration of people all over the world.

When Eleanor Roosevelt was a very young woman, she went to the slums of New York City to help children. Later, she visited coal mines and then campaigned to improve the terrible working conditions for miners. In fighting for the rights of minorities, she stood up to the powerful. In her later years, she led the fight for human rights throughout the world. She was a champion of the poor, a guiding light for the wretched, a voice for the downtrodden.

> **"In spite of timidity and fear, in spite of a lack of special talents, one can find a way to live widely and fully."**

Roosevelt was often attacked for her efforts to help the least fortunate members of society. She was called a do-gooder and worse. Even as First Lady, she was ridiculed at the highest levels of government, jeered at in Congress, made fun of in the newspapers. When she braved the dangers of wartime travel to make friends for the United States in faraway places, her enemies at home accused her of having communist sympathies. And in her last years, when she led the international fight for human rights, the charge was made again.

Eleanor Roosevelt wasn't a communist. She was a woman who had grown beyond her background. She had been raised at a time when her family and many other wealthy people held racist and anti-Semitic views. She grew to realize that such beliefs were wrong, and she fought against them. She had been taught that the rich were rich because they were smarter and worked harder than others, but she came to appreciate that other factors—such as greed, education, and luck—were also responsible. She was brought up to view women as inferior to men in their ability to reason. By the life she lived, she proved to herself and to the world how wrong that idea was.

A WOMAN OF CONTRADICTIONS

Eleanor Roosevelt lacked self-confidence but never backed away from standing up for her convictions. She was awkward but dignified, shy but persuasive. Her voice could be shrill, but her sincerity was overwhelming. Her principles were always unshakable. She believed that at heart people were good, but that sometimes they behaved badly. She believed that, like herself, they were imperfect but could always strive to be better. She believed that she had an obligation to leave the world a better place than she found it—and she did.

Eleanor Roosevelt was one of a kind. There has never been anybody quite like this person whom a political opponent called the "most remarkable and most energetic woman of her time." Others simply called her Eleanor, or ER, or Madame President. But before she was known by any of these names, she answered to the name Granny.

CHAPTER TWO

THE UGLY DUCKLING

The seeds of unhappiness are sometimes planted before one is even born, in the unhappy lives of parents or grandparents. That's how it was with Eleanor Roosevelt. Her grandfather, Valentine Hall, was the spoiled son of rich parents. As a young man, his drinking and gambling disgraced his family. He reformed himself, became devoutly religious, and married.

His wife, Mary Livingston Ludlow Hall, was ten years his junior, and he "always treated her like a child." Although much admired for her beauty, Mary Hall was a meek and dutiful wife who gave in to her husband's wishes in every respect. He even selected her clothes for her, as well as for their children. He ran a strict household and disciplined his children harshly. Hall even hired a clergyman to live in his house to enforce the rigid beliefs that he imposed on his family.

The Halls had two sons and four daughters. Their oldest child, Anna, was Eleanor Roosevelt's mother. Anna was often the target of her father's tyranny. One of Eleanor's sons once described how his grandmother "was strictly disciplined in mind and body." Her father "forced her to walk several times a day with a stick held in the crook of her elbows across her back in order to improve her posture."

Anna was only 17 years old when Valentine Hall died suddenly at age 46. His widow, who had always bowed to his wishes, had no experience in handling finances and running the household. She tried to maintain his strict standards, but her sons, Valentine III and Edward, were wild and hard to control.

Mary came to depend on young Anna for help in practical matters. But when Anna was 19, she left home to get married. Unable to manage her sons, Mary Hall nevertheless clung to her husband's beliefs in harsh discipline and strict religion. She sank deeper and deeper into a depression that would cloud the rest of her life.

A TRAGIC COUPLE

Like her mother, young Anna was much admired for her beauty. Her daughter, Eleanor, remembered her as "one of the most beautiful women I have ever seen." Anna herself considered beauty, charm, and grace the most important qualities a woman could have. Although Anna's stern upbringing had left her lacking warmth, Eleanor's father, Elliott Roosevelt, fell in love with her. They were married on December 2, 1883. The *New York Times* called the ceremony "one of the most brilliant weddings of the season."

Elliott Roosevelt was 23 years old when he wed 19-year-old Anna Hall. The Roosevelt family had been prominent in America from colonial times. Elliott was the younger brother of Theodore Roosevelt, who would one day be president of the United States. As a schoolboy, Elliott fought bullies who picked on Theodore, who was sickly. Although the brothers sometimes clashed, they always remained close.

At the time of his marriage, Elliott was known as a sportsman, an elephant hunter, and a Manhattan nightlife celebrity. He was one of the most popular young bachelors in New York society. But already, gossip swirled that he drank too much and sometimes behaved badly. Still, there was no doubt that he was head-over-heels in love

"I do not see how I can make her happy."

with Anna. "She seems to me so pure and so high and ideal," he sighed, that "I do not see how I can make her happy." He wondered how "any single love [could] make up for the lavish admiration of the many."

Their first child, Eleanor Anna Roosevelt, was born on October 11, 1884, less than a year after their wedding. Her father called Eleanor "a miracle from Heaven." She would describe him as "the love of my life."

ENTERING THE WORLD

Eleanor entered a world of high society, snobbery, and wealth. The world in the 19th century was very different from the one we know today. There were no cars, no airplanes, no computers, no VCRs, no televisions—not even electricity. The New York neighborhood where the Roosevelts lived was lit by gaslight. The streets were filled with the sounds of horses and wagons, and the cobblestones smelled of manure. Poor people lived in tenements without bathrooms, sometimes without windows. Many of them came down with deadly tuberculosis. Other diseases also devastated poor neighborhoods, and sometimes they spread to the rich as well.

It was a time when widespread prejudice against African-Americans and immigrants, particularly the Irish and the Jews, often exploded into violence. Rich people like the Roosevelts were

*Six-year-old Eleanor Roosevelt (right) poses with
her father Elliott Roosevelt and her two brothers
Elliott (far left) and Hall.*

outraged by the violence. Their own prejudices
were expressed more quietly and were enforced by
barring such outsiders from schools, clubs, and
businesses.

These attitudes were firmly planted in the
exclusive society in which Elliott and Anna
Roosevelt moved. Theirs was a world of lavish par-

ties and charity balls aswirl with evening gowns and formal men's wear. Night after night the scene was alive with furs and jewels lit by glittering chandeliers. There were amateur plays, scavenger hunts, theater parties, and late-night dinners. It was an elite world of handsome men and beautiful women like Elliott and Anna Roosevelt.

Anna loved the excitement, as well as the admiration her beauty attracted. Her nights were full of dancing and partying. Her days, however, were spent recovering. She sometimes felt drained and overtired. She did not much want to deal with an infant or, later, a growing child. In those days, there was no thought that a father might take on such duties.

Anna mostly left the care of Eleanor to nurse-maids. Eleanor would remember that her mother "made a great effort for me, she would read to me and have me read to her, she would have me recite my poems." Eleanor also recalled "the look in her eyes and hear the tone of her voice as she said: 'Come in, Granny.'" Once Eleanor overheard her telling a guest why she called her that. "She is such a funny child, so old-fashioned that we always call her 'Granny,'" Anna had explained.

> **"She is such a funny child, so old-fashioned that we always call her 'Granny.'"**

From the time she was very little, Eleanor felt that she could never please Anna. "I was always disgracing my mother," she recalled. Later, there was never any doubt that Anna preferred her two sons to her daughter. Elliott Jr. was born in 1889 when Eleanor was four years old. A second brother, Hall, arrived two years later.

Before the two boys were born, when Eleanor was still an only child, Elliott Roosevelt's drinking problems began growing worse. His marriage was in trouble, and in an effort to patch it up, he and Anna decided to go abroad. They took Eleanor, then two and a half years old, with them.

A FEARFUL CHILD

In the spring of 1887, the Roosevelts sailed out of New York on the ocean liner *Britannic.* The first day out, in a thick fog, their ship was struck by another steamship. The scene was sheer horror. Passengers and crewmen were injured. Many died. Lifeboats were lowered through the dense fog into a stormy sea.

Elliott helped Anna and Eleanor's nursemaid into a lifeboat while a sailor held onto Eleanor on the deck above them. All around Eleanor was noise and turmoil, confusion and terror. Elliott called to the sailor to drop the child into his waiting arms. But the terrified and screaming girl

*Eleanor and her brother Elliott sport
fashionable winter clothes.*

would not let go of the sailor. Finally he pried her
loose and dropped her to her father. For years
afterward, Eleanor had nightmares of hurtling
downward towards the sea-tossed lifeboat.

Over the next few years, she grew into a fearful child, as timid as she was awkward. Her father's love was the one thing she was sure of, and she returned it, but Elliott could not give her security. He was unstable. His drinking became more and more of a problem. He and Anna had loud quarrels, which Eleanor could not help over-hearing. These arguments made her feel even less secure.

Shortly before Eleanor's brother Elliott Jr. was born, her father broke his ankle. It was a silly accident. Elliott had been turning somersaults. The bone didn't set properly, and the ankle had to be rebroken and reset. Weeks of extreme pain fol-lowed. Doctors gave him morphine, a powerful drug that can be habit-forming. Elliott became addicted to it. Over the next few years, he used the drug regularly and continued to drink heavily.

By the time Eleanor's brother Hall was born, Elliott was completely in the grip of drugs and liquor and was threatening suicide. Anna was afraid for him and for herself and the children. She felt she could no longer cope with the situa-tion. Eleanor's uncle Theodore took charge of his younger brother. He declared that Elliott must stop drinking and taking drugs and laid down a set of rules to enforce the decision. Because Elliott's behavior towards his wife and children had been so threatening, Elliott was to stay away from them for two years. At the end of that time,

Eleanor's uncle, Theodore Roosevelt, was the 26th U.S. president (1901–9).

if he was drug- and alcohol-free, he would be allowed to rejoin them. To establish a distance between Elliott and his family, Theodore put his brother to work managing some property he owned in Virginia.

Seven-year-old Eleanor did not understand what was happening. Why could she no longer see the one person she knew truly loved her? She could not be comforted. Nor could she find the love she needed with her mother and two brothers. "I felt a curious barrier between myself and these three," she recalled later.

"I felt a curious barrier between myself and these three."

There were, however, some rare moments of closeness between Eleanor and her mother. These occurred when Anna suffered painful backaches and headaches marked by a dimming of her eyesight. When she took to her bed with the curtains drawn against the light, Eleanor would sit with her silently and gently rub her temples and tell her mother with her touch what neither of them could put into words.

The doctors could not identify Anna's illness. An exploratory operation was performed. Following it, she came down with diphtheria, a disease that affects the heart and nervous system. She fell into a coma that lasted for several weeks. Then, on December 7, 1892, shortly after Eleanor's eighth birthday, 29-year-old Anna Hall Roosevelt died.

TO GRANDMOTHER'S HOUSE

Eleanor and her two brothers were sent to live with their grandmother, Mary Hall. Her father's visits—he was drinking again—were held to a minimum. On one such visit he took Eleanor for a walk with three of his prize fox terriers. He handed her the dog leashes outside a men's club and told her to wait for him while he went inside for a moment. It was six hours before he emerged, so drunk that he had to be helped into a cab. Eleanor never forgot her feelings of having been abandoned and not knowing what to do. Her father loved her, but she could not depend on him.

Eleanor could rely on her grandmother, but Mary Hall suffered from a deep depression that kept her from showing love. In place of love she enforced the stern discipline and the strict religion that she had learned from her husband. During the day, Eleanor saw her rarely. Grandmother Hall emerged from her room only for morning and evening prayers. She established rules regarding Eleanor's daily schedule, the clothes she wore, and the friends she was allowed to see. Concerned about Eleanor's tendency to stoop, she made the child wear an uncomfortable steel back-brace for almost an entire year.

ALONE IN THE WORLD

Eleanor found little companionship in her brothers. Hall was still a baby looked after by a nursemaid, and Elliott Jr. was a toddler. She never really got to know him because Elliott Jr., not yet four years old, died of scarlet fever and diphtheria in May 1893. Nine-year-old Eleanor wrote her father that now her little brother would be "safe in Heaven" with their mother.

A year later, on August 13, 1894, Elliott Roosevelt wrote to Eleanor apologizing for not having visited or written her in such a long time. He said that he had been ill and confined to his bed but did not mention that he had recently taken a bad fall while drunk. After writing the letter he fell into a coma. A few hours after it was mailed, Elliott Roosevelt died. An orphan now, Eleanor was heartbroken. "Never forget I love you," her father's letter had assured her. Who was there left to love her now?

A GRIM CHILDHOOD

Eleanor was ten years old when her father died. She was living in her grandmother's mansion in

New York City with two aunts, two uncles, her three-year-old brother Hall, a governess, and a full staff of household servants.

It was not a happy house. Eleanor's 16-year-old aunt Maude was already following in the footsteps of 21-year-old aunt Pussie—staying out late at night, going to wild parties with older men, causing gossip. Eleanor's uncles, 25-year-old Vallie and 22-year-old Eddie, had well-earned reputations as heavy drinkers whose behavior was scandalous and—because they often carried guns—downright dangerous. Grandmother Hall had given up trying to control her children, but she was determined that Eleanor and Hall would be brought up with the strictest discipline.

Hall avoided much of this discipline when he was sent away to school. Eleanor worried about her little brother. "I write him every day," she told a schoolmate. "I want him to feel he belongs to somebody."

"I want him to feel he belongs to somebody."

Her concern for Hall would last throughout his life.

Eleanor did not escape the harsh discipline. Her governess, Madeleine, was a tyrant. If Eleanor made a mistake, she heaped scorn on her. Eleanor would always remember how Madeleine pulled her hair "unmercifully." A cousin of Eleanor's remembered the governess as "a terrifying character" and Eleanor's childhood as "the grimmest. . . . I have ever known." Eleanor's uncles Vallie and Eddie made it even more grim. She was often awakened by their late-night quarrels and drunken behavior. They could be nice to her, but she lived in fear of them, never knowing what they might do next.

Fearful, unsure of herself, and shy, Eleanor made no close friends. Some of the girls she knew laughed at her behind her back. As she entered her teens, her grandmother continued to dress her as a little girl. At an age when the other girls were wearing fashionably long dresses, Eleanor wore dresses with short skirts. They were shapeless and fell straight to just above her knees. Her black stockings and high-button shoes had not been in style for years.

Eleanor was awkward and quite tall for her age. Her teeth were in braces. Her aunt Edith, the second wife of her uncle Theodore Roosevelt, described Eleanor as "very plain. Her mouth and teeth seem to have no future." Edith also observed that "the ugly duckling may turn out to be a swan."

Grandmother Hall insisted that she attend dancing classes. Eleanor hated them because she knew how awkward she was and that she was not wanted as a partner. Even worse, as she grew older she was forced to attend formal dances and balls. When she was 14 years old, she went to a Christmas dance. Typically, her dress was too short and had unfashionable blue bows on the shoulders. Eleanor stood on the sidelines watching as her cousin Alice, Uncle Theodore's daughter, swirled past in a long gown, laughing with the handsome boy who was her partner. When the music stopped, Alice whispered something to the boy. He immediately came over and asked Eleanor for the next dance. Gratefully, she accepted the invitation of this charming 16-year-old. He was a distant cousin of hers named Franklin Delano Roosevelt.

FINISHING SCHOOL

Eleanor did not see Franklin again for almost five years. The year after they met, her life changed. Her mother had wanted her to go to boarding school abroad, and now Grandmother Hall decided to send her there. At age 15, Eleanor left for Allenswood, an exclusive girls' finishing school on the outskirts of London.

The head of the school was Marie Souvestre, a 70-year-old Frenchwoman. She was a strong person who was sympathetic to the poor and the downtrodden. She believed that the girls who came to her from wealthy families should leave with a sense of obligation toward those less fortu-

Students at Allenswood enjoy their leisure time. Eleanor began attending the exclusive British boarding school at age 15.

nate. Mademoiselle Souvestre insisted that her students exercise their minds and find their own meanings in what they had been taught.

Eleanor adored Madamoiselle Souvestre. On her first day there, she and the 34 other Allenswood students—most of them English— were told that they must speak only French. This was no hardship for Eleanor, who had learned to speak the language fluently from her French governess. At mealtimes, while the other girls stumbled over grammar, Eleanor carried on lively conversations with the headmistress. Eleanor assisted the other girls with their French, and for the first time in her life she found herself liked and respected. It was a dizzying feeling not only to be accepted but to be a leader of the class.

Along with a few other favored girls, Eleanor was invited to evenings in Madamoiselle Souvestre's study. They read and discussed poems and stories. They also discussed such current events as the Boer War, which was fought between the Dutch and the English for control of South Africa, and the U.S. elections—Eleanor's uncle Theodore was running for vice president. The headmistress had both charisma and a taste for unpopular causes. She "shocked me into thinking," Eleanor would remember later.

Eleanor's mind and personality blossomed. She gained self-confidence, became more outgoing, made friends, and even played on the school's field hockey team. During school holidays, Eleanor did not go home. On one occasion, she accepted an invitation to tour Europe with the headmistress. Eleanor learned to take responsibility for lodgings, meals, and train schedules and tickets. They went off the beaten track, observed the lives of ordinary people, strolled through slum neighborhoods, chatted with poor children in their native languages. Perhaps the most important lesson Madamoiselle Souvestre taught Eleanor was how to enjoy herself.

THE DEBUTANTE

When she was 18, Eleanor was summoned back to New York to make her debut into society. She was, after all, the niece of Theodore Roosevelt, now the president of the United States.

Eleanor settled in at Tivoli, Grandmother Hall's spacious home overlooking the Hudson River in upstate New York. The estate contained tennis courts, riding stables, hiking trails, and acres of green woodlands. But instead of enjoying these luxuries, Eleanor's days were filled with fear. Her uncles, Vallie and Eddie, were drunk all the time. They carried their rifles everywhere and fired them at random. Three strong locks were fastened to Eleanor's bedroom door as protection.

During that summer of 1902, Eleanor took a train to New York City to buy accessories to go with the Parisian gown that she would wear when she made her debut. Coming back, she was recognized by the distant cousin who had danced with her five years earlier. Now 20 years old, Franklin Roosevelt was more handsome and charming than ever. He sat next to Eleanor, and they chatted easily for almost two hours. They

College senior Franklin Roosevelt (seated, center) poses with members of the board of the Harvard Crimson *newspaper.*

parted knowing that they would surely see each other again.

Franklin Roosevelt did not attend the Assembly Ball at the Waldorf-Astoria Hotel where Eleanor made her debut. Despite her lovely gown, she considered the evening a total disaster. She was taller than most of the young men there, and they were slow to ask her to dance. She was conscious that older people were comparing her to her beautiful dead mother and shaking their heads. Eleanor left early.

HELPING THE NEEDY

Despite her unhappiness at society events, Eleanor was not timid regarding other activities. She joined the Junior League, a group of debutantes dedicated to helping the poor and needy. Acting on Marie Souvestre's teachings, Eleanor went to the slums of Manhattan's Lower East Side. She ignored the violence and danger in the streets and led classes for immigrant children in a settlement house (a center for social welfare).

The slums horrified and fascinated Eleanor, and her work there made her feel useful. She joined the Consumers League to study the working conditions of poor young women. She met scrubwomen and laundresses and factory workers whose take-home pay for a 72- to 84-hour week was $6. At the time, child labor was still legal in the United States. She visited sweatshops where she saw four- and five-year-old children working "until they dropped with fatigue."

Eleanor's charity work filled her days, but her evenings were less bleak. As a new debutante she was expected to go to a series of dances and balls. Ordinarily, Eleanor would have hated this. But things had changed for her. There was now a young man who could be depended upon to attend when she did. He danced with her, and they had long conversations. He was becoming more and more interested in her, and she in him. Eleanor's courtship by the handsome and dashing young Franklin Delano Roosevelt had begun.

CHAPTER THREE

MARRIAGE AND MOTHERHOOD

Handsome and dashing as he was, young Franklin Roosevelt was not popular with his schoolmates at Harvard. They thought him arrogant and made fun of the vaguely English accent he had picked up from the governesses who had raised him. He was not good at sports, and his eagerness to provide answers in class earned him a reputation as a know-it-all.

Franklin was the only child of Sara Delano Roosevelt, a widowed mother who had spoiled him. Until the age of five, he had long blond hair that was never cut and wore skirts. (It was common at that time for parents to clothe preschool boys in dresses.) He was nine years old before he was allowed to bathe himself without his mother present. Mother and son were very close and Franklin would be devoted to her—and often dependent on her—for as long as she lived.

His attachment to his mother was noticed by the young debutantes he met during his college years. While they recognized his charm and admired his good looks, they thought Franklin conceited, and they sensed that in his eyes they could never measure up to his mother.

Eleanor did not see him this way. She was impressed by his quick mind and lively conversation. She was comfortable with him and flattered by his attention.

Eleanor and Franklin began seeing more and more of each other. Franklin escorted her to parties. He took her boating. She was his date at the Harvard-Yale football game. They took long hikes together. It was a restrained relationship. In the early 1900s, courtship was not a contact sport. "The idea that you would permit any man to kiss you before you were engaged to him never even crossed my mind," said Eleanor.

A PROPOSAL

One Sunday she visited her brother Hall at Groton, an exclusive prep school for boys. Franklin had also attended Groton, and he followed her there. They took a long walk by themselves, and Franklin proposed marriage. "Why me?" Eleanor responded. "I am plain. I have little to bring you." But he assured her of his love, and she accepted his proposal.

Sara Delano Roosevelt was not pleased. Her son was the center of her life. She thought Franklin and Eleanor were too young to get married: he was 21 and she, 19. Sara made them promise to keep their engagement secret for at least a year. She took Franklin with her on a long cruise to the West Indies, hoping that the separation would end the relationship. She saw to it that Franklin spent time with one or another of the young women onboard ship. None of her strategies worked.

When they came back home, Sara tried to get Franklin a post with the U.S. ambassador to England so that he would again be separated from Eleanor. That too failed. Sara stalled a few more months but finally relented. The wedding took place on March 17, 1905. Eleanor was given away by her uncle Theodore Roosevelt, the president of the United States at the time. He was the center of attention that day, and Eleanor and Franklin felt neglected by their wedding guests.

Following a three-month honeymoon in Europe, they settled down in New York City, where Franklin attended Columbia University Law School. On May 3, 1906, their daughter, Anna Eleanor Roosevelt was born. She was the first of their six children. "For

"For ten years, I was always just getting over having a baby or about to have one."

Eleanor poses for a formal wedding photograph. She and Franklin were married on March 17, 1905.

ten years," Eleanor later sighed, "I was always just getting over having a baby or about to have one."

In December 1907, the Roosevelts' first son, James, was born. Franklin Jr., a second son, was born in March 1909. When he was seven months old, he was stricken with the flu. Franklin Jr. died the same year he was born. Eleanor blamed herself. "I felt that I had not cared enough about him," she wrote. "I made myself and all those around me most unhappy during that winter. I was even a little bitter against my poor young husband." Franklin escaped by plunging into his work at the law firm he had joined. Despite her bitterness, Eleanor soon became pregnant again. Another son, Elliott, was born on September 23, 1910.

SARA ROOSEVELT

Eleanor was not a happy mother. One major reason for this was her mother-in-law. From the first, Sara had dominated the marriage. She influenced Franklin in all matters, regardless of the effect on his wife.

Franklin did not make much money, and his mother provided an allowance so his young family could live comfortably. Sara often wrote checks to cover additional expenses. At her insistence, Eleanor gave up her work in the slums. Sara bought a lot on East 65th Street in New York City

In 1912, Eleanor and Franklin sit with their children (left to right) Anna, James, and Elliott.

and had twin houses built, each six stories tall. She moved into one, Franklin and Eleanor and their children into the other. Sara and Franklin planned the furnishings for his family's home; Eleanor was excluded.

One night Franklin found his wife sobbing in the bedroom. What's the matter? he wanted to know. "I don't like living in a house which is not in any way mine," Eleanor told him. "Don't be such a goose," was his response.

Franklin began to stay out late at night, dining with friends or playing poker at exclusive men's clubs. When he was home, he spent at least

Sara Roosevelt doted on her only son, Franklin, and made life miserable for her daughter-in-law, Eleanor.

as much time with his mother as with Eleanor and his children. Sara was always a presence in Eleanor's house, and Eleanor bowed to her judgment in most matters.

ENTERING POLITICS

The family spent holidays at Sara's Hyde Park estate in Dutchess County, New York. The Roosevelts had been prominent in the area since colonial times. Franklin had grown up here and was recognized as an up-and-coming young lawyer. He had developed a warmth to go with his natural charm. Dutchess County Democratic Party leaders asked him to run for the New York state senate, mainly because his mother could afford to finance his campaign.

Dutchess County had always been a solidly Republican district, but Franklin poured as much energy into the campaign as his mother did money. He crisscrossed the county by car, covering two thousand miles of dirt roads to convince back-country farmers to vote for him. His efforts succeeded. Franklin was elected.

Eleanor, Franklin, and the children moved to Albany, the state capital. Sara did not go with them. For the first time in her married life, Eleanor was out from under her mother-in-law's domination. The family moved into their Albany home on January 1, 1911, the day Franklin was sworn into office. The next day, Eleanor hosted an open house for her husband's fellow Democrats. It was her first encounter with the sometimes hard-drinking, cigar-smoking professionals who could make or break the career of a young politician. Many of these were rough-spoken men who used spittoons and sometimes missed. Eleanor was fascinated by them—and by politics.

She called on the wives of other state senators, and she entertained the big-city party leaders. Many of them found Franklin stuffy and conceited, but they liked Eleanor because she listened when they talked. When Franklin attacked these bosses and their hold on the Democrats, they denounced him as a traitor to the party. Eleanor played a key role in patching things up in time to secure their support for Franklin's reelection to the state senate in 1912.

In March of that year, Franklin went to Washington, D.C., for the inauguration of President Woodrow Wilson. There, he met Jonathan Daniels, whom Wilson had just appointed secretary of the navy. They discussed their mutual admiration for Theodore Roosevelt, Eleanor's uncle, who had once served as secretary of the navy. Franklin, a believer in the need for a strong navy, impressed Daniels, who offered Franklin the post of assistant secretary of the navy. Franklin accepted.

TO THE NATION'S CAPITAL

When Eleanor and the children joined Franklin in Washington, D.C., in the autumn of 1913, she was thrust into a whirlwind of social engagements. As the wife of an up-and-coming young member of the administration, she had to entertain frequently and make friends with important legislators. She kept track of upcoming bills affecting the Department of the Navy so she could discuss them intelligently and promote Franklin's interests among those who voted on them.

During all this activity, Eleanor became pregnant again. On August 17, 1914, the second Franklin Delano Roosevelt Jr. was born. By then, World War I had begun in Europe. The United States was not yet involved, but with German submarines in the Atlantic, the need to build up the navy was urgent. Eleanor worked behind-the-scenes to help Franklin achieve this.

The pressure did not let up over the next two years. In February 1916, Eleanor gave a party for 225 people important to naval funding. She was in her eighth month of pregnancy. She gave birth for the sixth time on March 13, 1916. Her

Eleanor joins Franklin and other U.S. Navy officials at the Navy Yard in New York City. Franklin served as assistant secretary of the navy for seven years (1913–20).

youngest son was christened John Aspinwall Roosevelt.

During this last pregnancy, Eleanor's paperwork—correspondence, invitations, scheduling updates—had piled up. She was overwhelmed and decided to hire a part-time secretary. She chose Lucy Mercer, a beautiful 23-year-old socialite. It was a pleasant change when Sara, down for a visit, approved the choice. "She is so sweet and attractive and adores you, Eleanor," she told her daughter-in-law. How bitterly those words would echo in Eleanor's memory!

As assistant secretary of the navy, Franklin was kept very busy after World War I broke out in Europe. His duties multiplied in April 1917, when the United States entered the war. Fortunately, he had the help of Louis Howe, a small man with a large capacity for work that matched his devotion to Franklin.

Howe, who had been with Franklin since his first state senate campaign, was a whiz at politics. He had seen Franklin as a rising star and hitched his wagon to him. Soon Franklin couldn't do without him and hired Howe as his private secretary. Throughout the years, Howe's loyalty to Franklin would never waver.

Eleanor didn't like Howe. She was offended by the way he made himself at home in her house, and she begrudged the amount of time he spent with Franklin. She resented being excluded from their political strategy sessions.

LIFE DURING WARTIME

With the United States' entry into the war, Eleanor became heavily involved with the Navy

Red Cross. She served doughnuts and coffee to sailors in a canteen in the wee hours of the morning. She was active with the Navy League and the Navy Relief Society.

During this time, Lucy Mercer took care of many of Eleanor's other obligations, responding to invitations and correspondence, organizing the dinner parties Eleanor had to give, paying household bills, and arranging and rearranging Eleanor's schedule. She was indispensable to Eleanor.

Eleanor's busy schedule left little time for her five children. They were being raised by nursemaids, governesses, and servants. She felt that she was neglecting them, and to some extent she surely was. She felt particularly guilty about Elliott. "He suffered for a great many years with a rather unhappy disposition," she wrote, adding that "in all probability I was partly to blame."

She tried to make up for her neglect of the children during summer vacations. Both before and after the war, these were spent at Campobello, an island off the coast of the Canadian province of New Brunswick. Sara had long owned a home there, and she built a house next to it for her son and his family. Here, aware that the warmth of motherhood did not come naturally to her, Eleanor devoted herself to her children as fully as she was able.

Franklin joined them at Campobello whenever he could get away from the pressures of his job. That wasn't as often as Eleanor would have liked. When he was there, he played with the children in an easy way that Eleanor could only envy.

THE CRUELEST BLOW

At the end of the summer of 1918, Eleanor and her children went to Hyde Park to visit Sara. Franklin was in Europe on navy business. World War I was drawing to a close, but an influenza epidemic raged throughout the world. It would claim the lives of 28 million people. On September 12, Eleanor received a telegram that Franklin had been stricken with influenza and was extremely ill. He was being treated on the ship bringing him back to the United States.

Eleanor and Sara met the vessel when it docked in New York. Franklin was alive, but many of the ship's crew who came down with the dread disease had been buried at sea. Although Franklin was still very ill, the physicians said that he would recover. He was brought to his mother's house on East 65th Street. The doctors gave him sedatives so that he could sleep.

As Eleanor unpacked his suitcase, putting his papers to one side, she noticed a large packet of letters. They were addressed to Franklin in a handwriting she could not help but recognize. They

Lucy Mercer began working as Eleanor's secretary in 1915. Eleanor eventually discovered that Franklin and Lucy were having an affair.

were love letters from Lucy Mercer. Her husband had been having an affair with her secretary.

Eleanor was devastated. They had been married for 13 years. They had five children. And now, it seemed, he was in love with a beautiful, younger woman. Sick as Franklin was, she confronted him. She was not willing to stay married to an unfaithful husband. If Franklin could not be true to her, then she wanted a divorce.

In those days of strict morality, divorce meant that Franklin would have immediately been fired as assistant secretary of the navy. Louis Howe persuaded Franklin that Eleanor was a political asset he could not do without. It was certain that the constitutional amendment giving the vote to women would pass in the very near future, and women would not be likely to vote for a man who had left his wife for a younger woman. A divorce would mean the end of any hope of a political career for Franklin.

Sara Roosevelt backed up Howe. Divorce was not to be considered. If Franklin left his wife and children for this other woman, she would cut him off without a cent. For the first time, Sara came down firmly on the side of her daughter-in-law. Franklin promised his mother and Eleanor that he would end the affair with Lucy Mercer. As noted by their son Elliott, Eleanor agreed to have Franklin "as a partner in public life, [but] not ever again as a husband." A little more than a year later, Lucy Mercer married another man.

ON THE CAMPAIGN TRAIL

By this time, February 1920, Louis Howe was busily promoting Franklin Roosevelt's political career. At the 1920 Democratic Convention, James M. Cox was chosen as the Democratic presidential nominee after a bitter contest. Roosevelt was selected as his running mate. He was approved unanimously by the convention delegates.

This event marked the start of Eleanor's participation in Franklin's career as more than just a hostess and behind-the-scenes helpmate. To attract the votes of women, who would be casting ballots in a presidential election for the first time in the country's history, Howe insisted that Eleanor be at Franklin's side when he crisscrossed the country making speeches.

The train rides between campaign stops were long and boring for Eleanor. Franklin would relax playing cards with members of his staff and reporters. Eleanor would read. Sometimes she would fall into conversations with Louis. He couldn't help knowing that she didn't like him, but he admired her intelligence and her ability to size up people. He made a point of discussing each day's events with her, running drafts of Franklin's speeches past her, and talking over campaign strategy. Slowly, Eleanor came to appreciate

Howe's political know-how and cleverness. His quick mind challenged her, and soon she was looking forward to their daily give-and-take. After the election was over, Eleanor missed those political conversations. Cox and Roosevelt were defeated by Warren Harding and Calvin Coolidge, who took 61 percent of the vote.

A SUDDEN ILLNESS

The following year, Eleanor and Franklin and the children went to Campobello Island for their usual summer vacation. One day, Franklin went swimming in the icy waters of the Bay of Fundy. That night he came down with a chill. By the next day he was running a high fever. He had back and leg pains and experienced difficulty moving his lower body. A local doctor was ferried to the island. He could not diagnose the illness. Eleanor had a specialist brought from Bar Harbor, Maine. By the time he arrived, Franklin could not move his body from the waist down. On August 25, 1921, the specialist diagnosed polio—then commonly known as infantile paralysis. There was no vaccine for polio at that time, and no known cure for the disease.

Campobello was a remote island that could be reached only by boat. The closest mainland medical facilities were not up-to-date. There were no

Eleanor and campaign workers are pictured on a passenger train car during the 1920 presidential campaign. Franklin was the Democratic candidate for vice president.

polio experts or treatment centers in the area, but during those early stages of the disease Franklin could not be moved. Three weeks passed before a specially trained nurse arrived to perform massage therapy. During that time, Eleanor cared for Franklin. She slept on a couch in his room to be there when he needed anything. She bathed him, massaged his back and lifeless legs, and saw to his most personal needs. She provided not just comfort but also the encouragement to help him fight off the despair of knowing he might never walk again.

Eleanor had always been at her best in times of trouble. Her life had been filled with such occasions. Illness and tragedy brought out the steel in her character. It was harder for Franklin. Eleanor's support was vital, but it was his own reserves of strength that kept him going when things seemed darkest. The mama's boy, the shallow charmer, the ambitious politician was now a man whose bravery was being tested for the first time. The depth of his valor impressed Eleanor. "Probably the thing that took most courage in his life was his meeting of polio," she recalled. "I never heard him complain. . . . . He just accepted it."

Franklin was finally moved to a hospital in New York and from there to their home in Manhattan. He was paralyzed from the waist down and his days were filled with painful and time-consuming exercises that didn't seem to help very much. He had a full-time nurse. Louis Howe moved in with the Roosevelts to take charge of Franklin's business and political affairs. With the five children and the servants, the house was so crowded that Eleanor had to share a room with her youngest son.

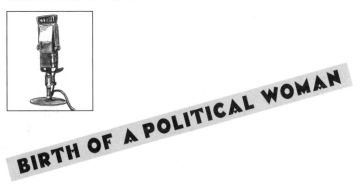

CHAPTER FOUR

BIRTH OF A POLITICAL WOMAN

Franklin's medical bills were staggering, wiping out the family's savings. Sara Roosevelt came to the rescue, paying their living expenses. Once again, they became dependent on Franklin's mother, which increased her control over their lives. Eleanor resented the situation and decided to earn money herself. She began to write articles on current topics for magazines. This led to speaking engagements and guest appearances on radio shows. As the wife of a popular Democrat who had run for vice president, she was much in demand.

Louis Howe was a great help to Eleanor. He saw her as the means of keeping Franklin's name before the public during his long recovery. Howe recognized that public speaking did not come easily to Eleanor. Her voice had a tendency to climb the scale and become shrill. Nervousness made her giggle. Louis spent countless hours helping her overcome such problems.

Howe went over her speeches, helping her sharpen the key points and teaching her to cut out excess words. He showed her how to break up her sentences so that they would be easier to deliver. He rehearsed her delivery with her, coaching her on how to stop for breaths and where best to pause. Howe also taught Eleanor to anticipate her giggles and to take deep breaths to avoid them.

He would sit in the back row of the hall when Eleanor spoke and make notes criticizing her performance. "Why did you give that silly giggle?" he would demand later. "Let's cut out the laughs and keep your voice down."

Eleanor was becoming known nationally through radio appearances, and she gained a reputation as a spokesperson for women. Louis urged her to join the women's division of New York State Democratic Committee. She quickly rose to a leadership position.

All this activity caused friction with her mother-in-law. In Sara's eyes, the political arena was no place for a lady. Indeed, ladies did not work at all. They stayed home and took care of their children. "When I began to earn money it was a real grief to her," Eleanor reported.

"When I began to earn money it was a real grief to her."

There was also conflict between Sara and Eleanor over Franklin's future. Sara thought that he should retire from politics permanently and move to Hyde Park, where he could live as an invalid gentleman and be looked after by her. Eleanor and Louis Howe were working tirelessly to make sure that Franklin would not be forgotten and that there would be opportunities for him when he was ready to resume his political career. Eleanor felt that this struggle with Sara changed her life. "She dominated me for years," she said. But the battle over Franklin's future, when he lay paralyzed with polio, "made me stand on my own two feet." Otherwise, she noted, "I might have stayed a weak character forever."

Franklin distanced himself from their differences. Throughout the early and mid-1920s, he focused on overcoming the crippling effects of polio. His doctors had advised lots of rest and relaxation and sunshine. At first, he went on deep-sea fishing expeditions in the warm waters off the coast of Florida. Later, he started spending time at a spa in Warm Springs, Georgia, where the waters were thought to be helpful in restoring power to paralyzed limbs and where expert massage and exercise programs were available. He would make regular visits to Warm Springs for physical therapy throughout his life.

Eleanor seldom joined Franklin on these

Franklin relaxes at Warm Springs, Georgia. Stricken by polio in 1921, he fought hard to overcome the crippling effects of the disease.

trips. Most of their time was spent apart. She was busy in New York with her new career. She was making new friends and political allies. In 1922, she met Nancy Cook, an assistant to the director of the Women's Division of the New York State

Democratic Party, and her friend Marion Dicker-
man. The three women began working together
during the week and spent frequent weekends
together at Hyde Park.

Franklin agreed to Eleanor building a cottage
for herself and her friends on the Hyde Park
property next to Val-Kill Creek. It would be far
from the main house and shielded by a grove of
woods. Eleanor, Nancy, and Marion would have
privacy there. Franklin worked closely with the
builders to ensure that Val-Kill would be just
what Eleanor wanted.

An experienced woodworker, Nancy Cook
built the furniture for the cottage herself. This so
impressed Franklin that he had another building
put up nearby that became a furniture factory.
The three women ran the factory, and the furniture was sold.

Construction of the cottage was finished by
1924, an election year. Eleanor had been writing
and speaking about such issues as the establish-
ment of an eight-hour working day, a minimum
wage law, education, health insurance, an end to
child labor, and the right of women to organize
into trade unions. Now she was active in having
some of these demands included in the platform of
the New York State Democratic Party.

She also led a group of politically active women
proposing similar resolutions to the national plat-

form committee at the 1924 Democratic National Convention, but they weren't passed. Nevertheless, Eleanor emerged as a force they would have to reckon with in the future.

A TRIUMPHANT RETURN

That same year, 1924, Franklin became active once again in politics. Louis Howe had worked hard to ensure that Franklin remained popular among the national party leaders in Washington. Eleanor's rise to power within the New York State Democratic Party had given her influence with Governor Al Smith. Eleanor and Louis persuaded Smith that Franklin Delano Roosevelt should nominate him as the party's candidate for president.

There were problems with this plan. For one, Franklin generally got around in a wheelchair. This was not the image that he wanted to present in his return to politics. The steel braces on his legs weighed seven pounds apiece. Using crutches, he had to drag his legs with each step. He was very concerned about how he would look getting from the entrance of the convention hall to the speaker's stand. He went to the hall early to practice. He used a crutch under his right arm and held on to the arm of his 16-year-old son, James, with his left hand. He taught James "to match his step to his own and copy his calm smile."

Franklin's speech nominating Al Smith was the high point of the convention, a personal triumph announcing that Franklin Delano Roosevelt was back in politics. The convention delegates, however, chose John W. Davis as the Democratic candidate. A dark horse unknown to many Americans, Davis lost the election to the Republican, Calvin Coolidge.

NEW EXPERIENCES

After the election, Eleanor continued her involvement in a variety of causes. She campaigned to end child labor, spoke out for equal education for boys and girls, and led a campaign to establish government-financed maternity and pediatric clinics and to set up health-care programs for mothers and infants. She successfully fought for measures to battle the high rate of infant deaths in the United States. When underpaid women factory workers went on strike in 1926, Eleanor joined their picket line. Police tried to break up the demonstration, but the women refused to move. Eleanor was arrested. The story made headlines.

More and more, Eleanor was opening herself up to new experiences. Although airplanes were then an uncommon and frightening way to travel, Eleanor was the first woman to fly at night. She took flying lessons from the famous female aviator Amelia Earhart.

In October 1927, Eleanor organized a women's peace movement to support the Kellogg-Briand Treaty to outlaw war. The following year, the treaty was signed by 63 nations, including the United States. She also opposed sending U.S. marines into Nicaragua, accusing the United States of "playing the part of the bully."

By 1928, Eleanor was a national figure with a solid base in New York Democratic politics. She was editor of the *Women's Democratic News,* on the board of directors of the Foreign Policy Association, director of the Bureau of Women's Activities of the Democratic National Committee, and the head of the Woman's Advisory Committee for Al Smith's second presidential campaign.

Her prominence had kept Franklin's name alive in politics. Meanwhile, Louis Howe had worked behind the scenes to further Franklin's career. Now their efforts paid off. In 1928, Franklin Roosevelt was nominated unanimously as the Democratic candidate for governor of New York.

A POLITICAL PARTNERSHIP

When Franklin was nominated for governor, Eleanor was not with him. She was traveling with the Al Smith presidential campaign. Asked by reporters what role she would play in her husband's race, Eleanor answered that she was busy with the national contest. During the weeks that followed, she took little part in Franklin's campaign.

Things changed when Smith lost to Republican Herbert Hoover and Franklin was elected governor by a narrow majority. Eleanor recognized that as the governor's wife, her political activities would reflect on him. She resigned from all of her Democratic Party posts, as well as from her leadership positions in other organizations. Now when she attended public functions, it was solely as her husband's representative.

The pattern of Eleanor and Franklin's political partnership began to emerge. Franklin could not move around the state easily because of his many duties and his paralysis. Eleanor traveled for him, identifying people's needs, clarifying problems, pinpointing issues, weighing the strengths and weaknesses of local elected officials, and measuring their support for Franklin's policies. She became his eyes and ears.

Eleanor inspected hospitals, asylums, and prisons. She talked to labor leaders and visited factories to observe working conditions. She reported to Franklin on pockets of rural poverty in upstate New York and on conditions in the slums of New York City, Buffalo, and Albany. She made recommendations to him on how state government might address people's needs.

The Roosevelts pose for a family portrait at their Hyde Park estate.

THE GREAT DEPRESSION

Eleanor's role became extremely important early in Franklin's term. On October 24, 1929, the stock market crashed, and the country's economy was shattered. As the Great Depression of the 1930s began, business failures and factory closings resulted in the loss of millions of jobs throughout the United States. Eleanor reported to Franklin that many of New York's working people were suddenly on the brink of poverty with homelessness and hunger very real dangers for large numbers of them. They needed help, and they needed it quickly.

President Herbert Hoover seemed unable or unwilling to help those who were hardest hit. Governor Roosevelt, on the other hand, pushed programs through the New York legislature that provided relief for those in the worst shape and jobs for many of the unemployed. As a result, he was reelected governor by a landslide in 1930.

At the same time that Franklin was becoming known nationally for his programs fighting the Great Depression, Eleanor was becoming well-known throughout the state as a sympathetic representative of the governor who would listen and help. She covered thousands of miles throughout the state, observing economic conditions and making recommendations on easing them. Many requests for help that came to the governor's mansion were addressed to her.

Eleanor refused to travel in a chauffeur-driven limousine. Instead, she drove herself in her own car. When she had some minor accidents, Franklin became concerned and assigned Earl Miller, a state trooper, to travel with her as escort and bodyguard. Miller was 32 years old, 12 years younger than Eleanor. He became devoted to Eleanor. He taught her to ride, to shoot, to dive, and to play tennis. They spent evenings reading poetry and novels aloud to each other.

They were together so much that it caused gossip. Were the rumors justified? Eleanor's son James thought they were. "I believe there may

Eleanor is pictured here with her chauffeur and friend, Earl Miller.

have been one real romance in mother's life outside of marriage," he wrote. "Mother may have had an affair with Earl Miller." He added, "if father noticed, he did not seem to mind."

Those closest to Eleanor and Franklin assumed that his paralysis ruled out any sexual relations. At the same time, there were whispers about him and his long-time secretary Missy LeHand. It may have been only a close working relationship with an emotional element, or it may have been more intimate than that. Elliott Roosevelt once walked in on his father "with Missy on his lap," and took for granted that they were lovers.

At any rate, LeHand was as invaluable in easing Franklin's workload during the last days of his second term as governor as Eleanor was. He was already recognized as one of six serious contenders for the Democratic nomination for president in 1932. Roosevelt had succeeded Smith as governor of New York, but he had not reappointed Smith's staff. Smith had never forgiven him and was determined that Roosevelt should not be nominated for president.

Smith's opposition was very hard on Eleanor, who had been one of Smith's closest allies. She tried to stay out of the conflict, but she was saddened when Smith joined forces with the conservative business interests that lined up against Franklin's policies.

Despite Smith's opposition, the Democratic National Convention nominated Franklin. A deal had been made, and for once Louis Howe had not been a part of it. Neither had Eleanor. To get the necessary votes for the nomination, Franklin had come out in opposition to the League of Nations and the World Court. These were both antiwar institutions that Eleanor had worked to promote. Eleanor was quietly furious. As Franklin's campaign against Herbert Hoover for the presidency began, she stopped talking to him.

CHAPTER FIVE

FIRST LADY

By 1932, the country was in the depths of the Great Depression. A third of the nation was ill-housed, ill-clothed, and ill-fed. Unemployed people were everywhere—on the long lines applying for the few jobs available, on the road moving from place to place in search of work, on the streets selling apples, and at the soup kitchens lining up for food. Whole families lived in shanty-towns of makeshift tents and tar-paper shacks with tin roofs. These were called Hoovervilles after Herbert Hoover. The president insisted that "conditions are fundamentally sound" and that "the fundamental strength of the nation's economy is unimpaired." With between 11 and 15 million people out of work, the country was not reassured.

Unemployed World War I veterans demanded help in the form of a bonus for their military service. Congress voted to give them the bonus but delayed paying it. Eleven thousand veterans marched on Washington and set up Hoovervilles, announcing that they would not budge until the bonus was paid. "Each day the men stage[d] a quiet, orderly vigil at the Capitol." On July 28, 1932, only a few weeks after Franklin Roosevelt accepted the Democratic nomination for president, federal troops armed with machine guns and tear gas set fire to the veterans' makeshift shanties and drove them out of Washington. One veteran was killed by city police and several others were injured. Hoover had ordered the raid.

A month later, Hoover announced that the "major financial crisis" was over. It wasn't. The American people had lost faith in their government, but there was a ray of hope in the person of Franklin Roosevelt.

Roosevelt spoke of attacking the Great Depression with new methods. If elected, he vowed to regulate the banks and the stock market, develop public works programs, provide unemployment insurance, and help farmers. He promised a "new deal" that would "restore this country to prosperity." Roosevelt campaigned tirelessly, crisscrossing the nation by train. Wherever he spoke, people were inspired by his energy and optimism. He brought hope to the hopeless.

Eleanor did not work directly on his campaign, but she was no longer punishing him for his opposition to the League of Nations. The problems of the Great Depression were too critical to waste time holding grudges. There was no doubt in Eleanor's mind that the welfare of the country depended on Franklin being elected.

Wherever she went, she spoke on his behalf. Whenever she was asked to appear on platforms with him, she did so. Most importantly, she spoke directly to the poorest Americans—to unemployed factory workers and farmers who had lost their land, to African-Americans in cotton fields and stoop laborers in lettuce patches, to coal miners and women with hungry children. Eleanor was becoming as well known as Franklin and because the times were so bad, her straightforward sympathetic manner was a great help to his campaign.

She remained outspoken. She cautioned New York state legislators against cutting the budget, warning them that if they cut jobs in the public works programs they would only have to pay more for unemployment relief. She said the result would be "people far more desperate than they have been up to now." She warned them bluntly: "If you and I were hungry, I doubt whether we'd be so patient as these people have been so far."

In November, Franklin was elected president by a landslide. He carried 42 of the 48 states. On March 4, 1933, he took office. "The only thing we

Eleanor and Franklin ride in a car during the 1933 inaugural parade. Solving the problems caused by the Great Depression was Franklin's top priority as president.

have to fear," he told the cheering inaugural crowd, "is fear itself."

THE FIRST HUNDRED DAYS

Eleanor stood beside Franklin as he took the oath of office. On one of her hands sparkled a sapphire ring, a gift. After the inauguration, she sent a letter to the giver. "I look at it," Eleanor wrote, "and I think she does love me."

The name of the giver was Lorena Hickock. She worked for the Associated Press and was considered the top woman reporter in the country when she was assigned to cover Eleanor during the campaign. A deep friendship had grown up between them. Eventually Hick, as she was called, quit her job with the Associated Press, took a position with the Democratic National Committee, and moved into the White House. She occupied a small room across the hall from Eleanor.

During the first hundred days of the Roosevelt administration, Eleanor, accompanied by Hick, went on one trip after another. Touring the country in a Plymouth convertible, Eleanor once again became Franklin's eyes and ears. To act effectively, he had to decide which of the many Great Depression problems were the most pressing. Eleanor traveled widely to identify them for him. She made recommendations on where government help was needed immediately and where it could wait. Although he didn't always follow her advice, it played an important part in his decisions. Franklin trusted Eleanor even when he didn't always agree with her.

Those first hundred days were marked by the introduction of one measure after another to fight the depression. Roosevelt closed the banks while

*In 1934, Eleanor enjoys a moment with her
close friend Lorena Hickok and Paul Pearson,
governor of the U.S. Virgin Islands.*

steps were taken to keep them from failing. He
pushed a bill through Congress that refinanced
mortgages to keep banks from foreclosing on farm
property and put a ceiling on the interest that
could be charged. He successfully sponsored a $3

billion public works bill, which led to a massive jobs program and stimulated the economy. Almost immediately, according to American Federation of Labor statistics, 1.6 million new jobs were created.

The depression was a long way from over, but there was hope in the country now. Eleanor went everywhere to see how the programs were working and to report back to Franklin. She visited

In 1935, Eleanor begins her descent into an Ohio coal mine. Throughout Franklin's presidency, she traveled widely to observe firsthand the social and economic conditions of the country.

slum dwellers in Puerto Rico and coal miners in Appalachia and sharecroppers in Arkansas. She spoke to the workers as well as the administrators. She visited prisons and chain gangs and poorhouses and infirmaries and orphan asylums. Eleanor poked into stew pots, sniffed at food bins, and asked countless questions. Franklin's political enemies called her a snoop and a busybody, but she gave the people the feeling that someone who had the president's ear was telling him where they hurt and how they might be helped.

After Hoover left office, the veterans returned to Washington, D.C., to again demand their bonuses. President Roosevelt opened an old army camp to house them and ordered that they should be given food and medical care. Eleanor went to visit them. She told the press they were "grand-looking boys with a fine spirit." One of the bonus marchers marveled that while "Hoover sent the Army, Roosevelt sent his wife."

"MY DAY"

Eleanor's popularity grew when she began writing a daily syndicated newspaper column called "My Day." She also wrote a monthly column for a magazine. Then she began speaking regularly on the radio.

By the end of Franklin's first term, she was

Eleanor gives an address over the NBC radio network. In addition to speaking regularly on the radio, she wrote a daily newspaper column and a monthly magazine column.

known all across the country as a do-gooder, unashamed of her concern for the underprivileged. Franklin, who came from a wealthy and distinguished family, was hated by some as a traitor to his class because of the liberal programs he had put in place. Eleanor was derided as a bleeding heart who was always on the road, rather than at home where a good wife should be, and as a buttinsky who had been elected to no office but nevertheless seemed to be running the country.

The majority of Americans did not share this view. When Franklin ran for a second term in 1936, Eleanor campaigned with him. He carried all but one state in the election, defeating his Republican opponent, Governor Alfred M. Landon of Kansas, by 11 million votes.

During the early years of Franklin's second term, Eleanor zeroed in on the plight of working women. With the Great Depression still in full swing, more than two million such women were still unemployed. Most jobs created by New Deal programs had gone to men. Eleanor campaigned for and got work relief programs for women. She also became the target of a wide variety of male journalists, politicians, and clergymen who were against women working no matter how great their need. She had always been a friend of labor, but now some labor unions also attacked her for taking jobs away from men.

EQUAL RIGHTS

African-Americans were the group hardest hit by the Great Depression. Many lived in the rural South, where they worked on farms or as share-croppers. The few who owned small farms were wiped out by the collapse of food prices. Many African-Americans sought work in northern cities only to find that blacks were the last hired and first fired. They were at the bottom of the bottom of the depression heap.

Eleanor invited a group of black leaders to the White House to discuss the plight of African-Americans. She listened sympathetically and took notes. The meeting lasted until after midnight, when the president came in to speak to the group. Franklin, however, found himself in a political bind. Since the Civil War, African-Americans had voted for the Republican Party of Abraham Lincoln. In 1932 they voted for Herbert Hoover, while white southerners voted solidly for Roosevelt. The South had elected a solid bloc of Democratic congressmen in favor of segregation. Roosevelt needed their votes to push through his New Deal legislation. As sympathetic as he was to the predicament of black Americans, he couldn't afford to lose southern white support.

Although the president's hands were tied, Eleanor's weren't. In 1933, lynchings (illegal executions by mobs) had claimed the lives of 24 black men. Early in 1934, Walter White, the head of the National Association for the Advancement of Colored People (NAACP), persuaded her to speak out in favor of a federal anti-lynching law. She recognized that Franklin couldn't come out publicly for such a bill, but she got him to promise that he would sign the bill if Congress passed it. A filibuster—a tactic allowing legislators to hold the floor by continuing to talk—by southern senators, however, prevented the bill from coming to a vote.

Eleanor was accused of making herself "offensive to Southerners by a too great affection for Negroes." This showed how thoroughly she had overcome her background. Her father's mother had been a southern belle, and Eleanor had been raised to believe in white supremacy. Throughout her early years, the only black people she had known were servants, whom she had called "my darkies."

Now Eleanor saw African-Americans as fellow human beings. She was shocked by how they were treated. In Washington, D.C., the nation's capital, they could not eat in many restaurants, were barred from many public and private schools, and were turned away from hotels. Throughout the South, they were not permitted to vote and had to sit in the back rows of balconies in movie theaters

In 1934, Eleanor addresses a conference on improving education for African-Americans.

and in the back of buses. In the armed services, blacks were segregated from whites.

Eleanor campaigned for regulations ensuring that African-Americans were not excluded from New Deal programs. She pressured officials to include blacks in the education seminars of the Federal Emergency Relief Administration. She fought for equal wages for black workers in government-financed projects. She made sure that relief funds were distributed in the black slums of Washington, D.C.

Eleanor soon had become an outspoken champion of civil rights. She met regularly with many African-American leaders. This upset some top presidential advisers. Eleanor wrote that they were afraid "I might hurt my husband politically." Franklin did not always do what she recommended, but neither did he interfere with her ongoing civil rights crusade.

In 1939, Eleanor attended the Southern Conference for Human Welfare in Birmingham, Alabama. She sat next to an African-American friend. A police officer told her that she was breaking the law, that blacks and whites had to sit on different sides of the center aisle. Eleanor had her chair moved to the middle of the center aisle. Thus, she was not breaking the law, but she was still refusing to segregate herself with the other whites. This attracted widespread newspaper coverage and national attention. "Her action," wrote New Deal historian Joseph P. Lash, "electrified black America. A National Congress of Negro Youth . . . . enthusiastically passed a resolution thanking her for her moral courage in Birmingham."

TRUE DAUGHTER OF THE
AMERICAN REVOLUTION

Eleanor's best-known stand for civil rights followed soon afterward. It involved Marian Anderson, an African-American woman who was the leading concert singer in the United States. Most halls were not large enough to hold the audiences that she attracted, but Constitution Hall in Washington, D.C., had enough seats. The Daughters of the American Revolution (DAR), a group of socially prominent white women who traced their ancestry back to the founding fathers, owned Constitution Hall.

Washington, D.C. was then (as it is now) a city with a majority black population, so a sell-out black audience for Marian Anderson was assured. The DAR, however, refused to rent their auditorium. "No Negro artist," vowed the president of the organization, "would be permitted to appear there." This announcement outraged the African-American community. Musicians, black and white, voiced their protest. Soon, groups of performers, artists, and writers all across the United States were condemning the discrimination.

Eleanor was a member of the DAR. Men on both sides of her family had fought in the American Revolution. Nevertheless, she acted.

"To remain as a [DAR] member," she wrote in her widely syndicated column, "My Day," "implies approval of that action, and therefore I am resigning." Her resignation made headlines around the globe. According to NAACP President Walter White, it "focused world-wide attention on the episode." Most importantly, a Gallup Poll showed that 67 percent of the American people approved of the First Lady's stand. It was a major victory for civil rights.

There was an immediate appeal to make the Lincoln Memorial available for an open-air concert by Marian Anderson. President Roosevelt gave his approval. Some 75,000 people, the majority of them black, attended the performance. Anderson opened with "America." Her final number, sung in a deep contralto voice that sent shivers through the crowd, was "Nobody Knows the Trouble I've Seen."

WORLD WAR II

In September 1939, German troops invaded Poland, and World War II began, as France, England, and, later, Russia, declared war against Germany, Austria, and Italy. Just about every other country in Europe became involved, and the war spread over Africa and Asia. During the first two years of the war, the United States did not fight.

The war challenged Eleanor's pacifist beliefs. In 1934, she had told a peace conference that they "must think of the next war as they would of suicide." In 1936, she spoke over the radio for the Quakers' Emergency Peace Campaign. She was the keynote speaker at the No-Foreign-War Crusade in 1937. By 1939, however, she had to ask herself if pacifism in the face of Nazi aggression was not just surrender.

Franklin was walking a tightrope, balanced between neutrality and preparedness. As president, he had to make sure the country could protect itself. He had to pressure Congress to spend money to beef up the military. Most Americans were against U.S. involvement in a European conflict. "Your boys," he told American parents in 1940, "are not going to be sent into any foreign wars." When he made that speech he was running for his third term as president. No other president had served more than two terms. Nevertheless, the American people overwhelmingly reelected Franklin over his Republican opponent, Wendell Willkie.

During the campaign, Eleanor had made anti-Nazi statements. Many thought the First Lady was pushing the country closer to war. Willkie supporters had made Eleanor an issue. They handed out millions of buttons proclaiming, "We Don't Want Eleanor Either."

Eleanor had also been involved in sponsoring a bill to ease immigration laws so that German-Jewish refugee children would be allowed to enter the country. The Quakers had arranged for families to take them in. Many people thought this proposal would involve the United States too closely in European affairs. Some labor unions on the left and America First groups on the right wanted to tighten immigration restrictions, not loosen them. Anti-Semitism reared its ugly head. Although the president supported the immigration bill, Congress did not pass it. "What has happened to us in this country?" Eleanor asked in "My Day." "We have always been ready to receive the unfortunates from other countries. . . . . We have profited a thousandfold by what they have brought us."

Throughout 1940 and 1941, Franklin became increasingly concerned with foreign affairs. The Japanese occupied large parts of China. Poland had been quickly defeated, and the German army seized France. The defeated British army retreated from Europe. Germany invaded Russia. The question had to be asked: Could the United States survive in a world ruled by Nazis?

President Roosevelt persuaded Congress to pass the first peacetime draft in U.S. history. He worked out a deal to sell England old U.S. destroyers and much-needed weapons. America

In 1941, Eleanor speaks to a group of striking electrical workers in Brooklyn, N.Y.

was, he said, "the great arsenal of democracy." Although Eleanor was fearful for all four of her sons who were now in the military, she supported these positions.

It was a difficult time in Franklin and Eleanor's personal lives. The passing of Franklin's mother, Sara, was followed by the tragic death of Eleanor's brother, Hall Roosevelt. Like their father, Hall had died of alcoholism.

WAR AGAIN

On December 7, 1941, the Japanese bombed Pearl Harbor, an American naval base in Hawaii, and the United States entered the war. Franklin asked Eleanor to serve as codirector of the Office of Civilian Defense. It was the only government post that she held during her husband's presidency. Franklin's political enemies protested. They could not attack the president in wartime, but his do-gooder wife was fair game. Not wanting to cause problems for Franklin, Eleanor resigned. Franklin then asked her to go to England and report back to him on conditions there. Her presence in London during air raids gave a tremendous boost to English morale.

In 1943, Eleanor traveled 23,000 miles to visit U.S. troops in the South Pacific. She went to Australia, New Zealand, and 17 other islands. According to Admiral William Halsey, when Eleanor visited wounded servicemen she "accomplished more good than any other person, or any group of civilians, who had passed through my area."

The pressures of war took their toll of Franklin. His once boundless energy was wearing thin. By 1944, the tide of battle was turning. U.S. and British troops had triumphed in North Africa and were marching through Italy. In the South Pacific, U.S. forces were winning back island after

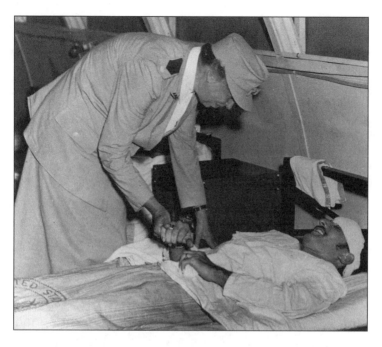

*During her 1943 trip to the South Pacific,
Eleanor comforts a wounded U.S. soldier.*

island from the Japanese. In June, a massive
Allied army landed on the coast of France and
began fighting its way inland. Franklin had
helped plan and coordinate these operations. He
also met with other world leaders to set up an
organization to prevent future world wars.

At the same time, problems at home had to be
resolved. This was Franklin's burden as he ran for
and won a fourth term. The strain was terrific. He

became thin and drawn and prey to illness. Franklin valued Eleanor's input, but he often didn't have the strength to deal with her. She had strong views on the postwar world. She wanted to be sure that children everywhere were protected. She wanted all the world's women to have equal rights. Franklin didn't disagree, but there were times he just wanted to relax.

A TERRIBLE LOSS

Franklin often went to Warm Springs, Georgia, to get away from the pressures. He was there on April 12, 1945, as the war in Europe was winding down. Eleanor was in Washington giving a speech when she was summoned back to the White House and received the news that Franklin had died of a stroke. She notified her four sons in the military. Then she broke the news to Vice President Harry

"Is there anything we can do for you? For you are the one in trouble now."

S. Truman. He asked if there was anything he could do for her. Eleanor told him no, adding "Is there anything we can do for you? For you are the one in trouble now."

After Truman was sworn in as president, Eleanor left for Warm Springs. When she arrived there she learned that Lucy Mercer Rutherford had been with Franklin when he died. He had been seeing her regularly for the more than 20 years since he had promised to end their affair. During Eleanor's frequent absences, Lucy had

On April 15, 1945, Eleanor (far left) looks on as Franklin's casket is lowered into his grave on the Roosevelt estate.

visited Franklin at the White House. "The butler would serve tea, close the door, and leave the President and Mrs. Rutherford alone," remembered chief White House usher J. B. West.

Eleanor's daughter, Anna, had served as hostess at White House dinners that Lucy had attended. Anna had known about the relationship and helped hide it from her mother. To Eleanor it seemed as if everybody knew except her. She managed to overcome her anger. She understood her duty as the president's wife, and, as always, she did it. Eleanor boarded her husband's funeral train and accompanied President Franklin Delano Roosevelt on his last journey to Washington.

CHAPTER SIX

A CHAMPION FOR HUMAN RIGHTS

On May 7, 1945, only 25 days after the death of President Roosevelt, Germany surrendered and the war in Europe was over. Broadcasting over radio station WNBC, Eleanor urged the people of the United States to struggle for peace as forcefully as they had fought the war. "Win through to a permanent peace," she told them. "That was the main objective that my husband fought for."

Japan surrendered on August 14, 1945, bringing World War II to an end. Four months later, President Truman appointed Eleanor as a delegate to the first meeting of the United Nations (UN) General Assembly in London. The Senate approved her appointment along with the appointments of four other delegates—all men. Each member of the delegation was assigned to a specific UN committee. Without consulting her, the men put Eleanor on Committee Three. That committee dealt with cultural, educational, and humanitarian concerns, rather than with matters the men considered important, such as politics and economics. Eleanor felt she was being discriminated against because she was a woman, but, she later wrote, she "agreed to serve where I was asked to serve."

Committee Three turned out to be a battleground between the United States and the Soviet Union, which was represented by Andrei Vishinsky. The issue was what to do with the millions of people in refugee camps throughout Europe. In the Soviets' view, there were only two kinds of refugees: those who wanted to go back to their homelands and "traitors, war criminals or collaborators." Eleanor, however, recognized a third group: people who had been both anti-Nazi and anticommunist and who would likely be executed if forced to return home. Eleanor viewed the Committee Three meetings as "one long wrangle." But in the end, she prevailed over the skilled speaker and diplomat Vishinsky. The UN Assembly decided that refugees would have a choice about where to settle.

On April 29, 1946, she was elected chairperson of the UN Commission on Human Rights. The commission was charged with drafting a Declaration of Human Rights that would apply to people worldwide. Eleanor drew up a framework emphasizing "personal rights, such as freedom of speech, information, religion, and rights of property; procedural rights, such as safeguards for persons accused of crime; social rights, such as the right to employment and social security, and the right to enjoy minimum standards of economic, social, and cultural well-being; political rights, such as the right to citizenship and the right of citizens to participate in their government."

In September 1947, Eleanor listens a speech at the United Nations General Assembly. At the time, she was serving as chairperson of the UN Commission on Human Rights.

In December 1948, after two years and eight months of work, the UN General Assembly adopted the Declaration of Human Rights. The vote was 48 to 0. The assembly gave Eleanor a standing ovation for her tireless work on the declaration. "She has raised a great name to an even greater honor," said the president of the assembly.

Eleanor served at the UN throughout the Truman administration but resigned when President Dwight D. Eisenhower took office. From 1953 on, she continued with her column and radio broadcasts, wrote articles for magazines, and was an active supporter of the Girl Scouts of America. She divided her time between an apartment in New York and the Val-Kill cottage at Hyde Park. Much of her time was spent with Lorena Hickock, who had taken an apartment in Hyde Park village to be close to Eleanor. In 1954 they collaborated on a book, *Ladies of Courage.* They would remain devoted to each other as long as Eleanor lived.

Throughout the 1950s, Eleanor continued to be active in public affairs. She championed U. S. support for Israel and continued to be an outspoken supporter of civil rights for African-Americans. Always a world traveler, in the 1950s she toured Europe, South America, the Middle East, Asia, Indonesia, and the Philippines.

In 1957, at age 73, Eleanor went to the Soviet Union as a correspondent for the *New York Post.*

She toured the country from Moscow to Samarkand, talking to ordinary people through an interpreter. When she returned, she lectured at Brandeis University on her Soviet tour and other topics of current interest. At the same time, she started a TV series called *The Prospects of Mankind.* Dr. Martin Luther King Jr. was the program's first guest.

President John F. Kennedy reappointed

At the 1960 Democratic National Convention, Eleanor basks in the audience's applause.

Eleanor as a delegate to the United Nations in 1961. He also named her to the Advisory Council of the Peace Corps. When Kennedy established a Commission on the Status of Women, he chose Eleanor to head it. She took these positions seriously and worked hard at them. Coworkers were always impressed by her knowledge and output. Problems seemed only to spark Eleanor's energy.

In 1962, she began work on a new book, *Tomorrow Is Now.* She never finished it. On November 7, 1962, Eleanor Roosevelt suffered a stroke and died at the age of 78. "Life was meant to be lived," she had written shortly before she died, "and curiosity must be kept alive. One must never, for whatever reason, turn his back on life."

"Life was meant to be lived."

They were words to live by, and Eleanor Roosevelt had indeed lived by them.

THE LEGACY OF ELEANOR ROOSEVELT

It has been more than three decades since Eleanor Roosevelt died, but her struggle continues. The victories she achieved during her lifetime were only stepping-stones to a better world. Many of the battles that Eleanor Roosevelt fought are still not completely won. The Human Rights

Declaration covers all the world's people, but making those rights a reality is an ongoing struggle. Child labor has been outlawed in the United States, but it continues in the poorer nations of the world. U.S. workers are guaranteed a minimum wage but are losing jobs to countries where pay is below the poverty level. African-Americans can no longer be barred from voting, eating in restaurants, staying at hotels, or sitting in the front of buses, but they still face discrimination in other spheres of life. Women have made advances in education, business, and politics, but their progress is restricted by enduring traditions and prejudice. There has not been another world war, but devastating conflicts, such as those in Bosnia and Rwanda, continue to break out.

Basic human rights, the protection of children, a minimum wage, equality for African-Americans and women—these were only some of the causes Eleanor championed. Her involvement sets an example for us all.

Despite growing up in a wealthy family, she felt the pain of the poor, understood their problems, and fought to do something about them. Despite being raised to view other races and religions as inferior to her own, she dealt with people as individuals. In doing so, she came to appreciate that African-Americans, Jews, Catholics, and others were victims of prejudice and were being denied equality. She spent much of her life fighting such bigotry.

Eleanor considered herself a pacifist, only suspending that position in the face of Nazi aggres-

Decades after her death, Eleanor Roosevelt endures as an admirable role model.

sion. Later she was in the forefront of the campaign to make peace in the world a reality.

As a turn-of-the-century woman, Eleanor had been expected to fill a narrow role as homemaker, wife, and mother. Instead, she carved out a place for herself and earned the world's admiration. Living proof of the capabilities of women, she set the standard for those women who followed her.

Although she was an idealist, she learned early in life that to change things one has to be practical. She accepted small gains and put her faith in the ongoing struggle. She recognized that the struggle would outlive her and understood that the hope of the world lay with future generations. She passed the torch to young people who have the future before them.

"You have to take defeat over and over again, and pick up and go on."

"You cannot get discouraged too easily," she advised them. "You have to take defeat over and over again, and pick up and go on."

The struggle to make the world a better place will always be worth the effort. It's the only world we've got. That struggle is the legacy of Eleanor Roosevelt.

A NOTE ON SOURCES

I used a number of sources in researching and locating quotations for this book. I consulted the leading biographies of Eleanor Roosevelt, which include *Eleanor Roosevelt: Volume One, 1884–1933* by Blanche Wiesen Cook (New York: Viking, 1992), *Eleanor, The Years Alone* by Joseph P. Lash (New York: Norton, 1972, and *Eleanor Roosevelt: A Life of Discovery* by Russell Freedman (New York: Clarion, 1993. In exploring the relationship of Eleanor and Franklin Roosevelt, *An Untold Story, The Roosevelts of Hyde Park* by Elliott Roosevelt and James Brough (New York: Putnam, 1973), *Eleanor and Franklin* by Joseph P. Lash (New York: New American Library, 1973), and *No Ordinary Time: Franklin Roosevelt and Eleanor Roosevelt—The Home Front in World War II* by Doris Kearns Goodwin (New York: Simon & Schuster, 1994) provided many insights. *Upstairs at the White House: My Life with the First Ladies* by J. B. West (New York: Warner, 1974), *Current Biography* (New York: H. H. Wilson, 1949), and *Chronicles of the Twentieth Century* (Mt. Kisco, NY: Chronicle Publications, 1987), and *Familiar Quotations, John Bartlett,* 16th ed., edited by Jonathan Kaplan (Boston: Little, Brown, 1992) helped fill in many of the historical and biographical details.

FOR FURTHER READING

Bode, Janet. *Beating the Odds.* New York: Franklin Watts, 1991.

Cook, Blanche Weisen. *Eleanor Roosevelt: Volume One, 1884–1933.* New York: Viking Penguin, 1992.

Faber, Doris. *The Life of Lorena Hickock: ER's Friend.* New York: William Morrow, 1980.

Freedman, Russell. *Eleanor Roosevelt: A Life of Discovery.* New York: Clarion Books, 1993.

Goodwin, Doris Kearns. *No Ordinary Time: Franklin and Eleanor Roosevelt—The Home Front in World War II.* New York: Simon & Schuster, 1994.

Hickock, Lorena A. *Eleanor Roosevelt: Reluctant First Lady.* New York: Dodd, Mead, 1980.

Larsen, Rebecca. *Franklin D. Roosevelt: Man of Destiny.* New York: Franklin Watts, 1991.

Lash, Joseph P. *Eleanor and Franklin.* New York: New American Library, 1973.

Lash, Joseph P. *Eleanor: The Years Alone.* New York: Norton, 1972.

Morgan, Ted. *FDR: A Biography.* New York: Simon & Schuster, 1985.

Roosevelt, Eleanor. *The Autobiography of Eleanor Roosevelt.* New York: Harper & Row, 1961.

Roosevelt, Eleanor. *Tomorrow Is Now*. New York: Harper & Row, 1963.

Schuman, Michael A. *Franklin D. Roosevelt: The Four Term President*. Springfield, NJ: Enslow, 1996.

Stewart, Gail B. *The New Deal*. Columbus, OH: Silver Burdett, 1993.

CHRONOLOGY

1884	Eleanor Roosevelt is born on October 11.
1892	Anna Roosevelt, Eleanor's mother, dies at age 29.
1894	Elliott Roosevelt, Eleanor's father, dies at age 34.
1905	Eleanor and Franklin Roosevelt are married.
1906	Eleanor and Franklin's first child, Anna, is born.
1907	Their second child, James, is born.
1909	Their third child, Franklin Jr., is born; he dies seven months later.
1910	Another son, Elliott, is born.
1911	Franklin Roosevelt is elected a New York state senator.
1913	Franklin Roosevelt is appointed assistant secretary of the navy.
1914	Another son, Franklin Roosevelt Jr., is born.
1916	Another son, John Roosevelt, is born.
1920	Franklin Roosevelt runs as the vice-presidential candidate of the Democratic Party.

1921	Franklin Roosevelt is stricken with infantile paralysis.
1922	Eleanor Roosevelt begins to make public speeches.
1922	Eleanor Roosevelt becomes involved in Democratic Party politics.
1924	Eleanor Roosevelt presents resolutions on women's issues to the Democratic Party Platform Committee.
1926	Eleanor Roosevelt is arrested for picketing with strikers.
1927	Eleanor Roosevelt organizes a women's peace movement to support the Kellogg-Briand Treaty.
1928	Franklin Roosevelt is elected governor of New York; Eleanor Roosevelt heads the Woman's Advisory Committee for Al Smith's second presidential campaign.
1930	Franklin Roosevelt is reelected governor of New York.
1932	Eleanor Roosevelt meets Lorena Hickock.
1932	Franklin Roosevelt is elected U.S. president.
1933–36	Eleanor Roosevelt travels around the country to study the effects of the Great Depression and report back to her husband.
1936	Franklin Roosevelt is reelected to a second term as president.
1937	Eleanor Roosevelt is the keynote speaker of the No-Foreign-War Crusade.
1937–39	Eleanor Roosevelt seeks government help for working women and equal rights for African-Americans.
1939	Eleanor Roosevelt resigns from the Daughters

	of the American Revolution in protest of their discrimination against African-Americans.
1940	Eleanor Roosevelt sponsors immigration bill to admit refugee children; Franklin Roosevelt is reelected to an unprecedented third term as president.
1942	Eleanor Roosevelt is appointed codirector of the Office of Civilian Defense, but political opposition forces her to resign.
1943	Eleanor Roosevelt visits U.S. troops in the South Pacific.
1944	Franklin Roosevelt is elected to a fourth term as president.
1945	Franklin Roosevelt dies on April 12.
1945	Eleanor Roosevelt broadcasts a victory message to American people; President Truman appoints her a delegate to the first meeting of the United Nations General Assembly.
1946	Eleanor Roosevelt is elected chairperson of the UN Commission on Human Rights.
1948	Human Rights Declaration is adopted by the UN; Eleanor Roosevelt receives a standing ovation for her leadership in drafting it.
1953	Eleanor Roosevelt resigns her UN post.
1957	Eleanor Roosevelt tours the Soviet Union as a correspondent for the *New York Post*.
1961	President Kennedy reappoints Eleanor Roosevelt as a UN delegate and as head of the Commission on the Status of Women.
1962	Eleanor Roosevelt dies on November 7 at age 78.

INDEX

Page numbers in *italics* indicate illustrations.

ABOUT THE AUTHOR

Ted Gottfried is the author of more than 50 books, both fiction and nonfiction, including biographies of Alan Turing, Enrico Fermi, and James Baldwin. Mr. Gottfried has taught writing at New York University, Baruch College, and other institutions. He is married and lives in New York City.